Martin Luther King, Jr.

Dr. Martin Luther King, Jr.

Remember.

by Marion Dane Bauer
Illustrated by Jamie Smith

SCHOLASTIC INC.

New York   Toronto   London   Auckland
Sydney   Mexico City   New Delhi   Hong Kong

ISBN-13: 978-0-545-14233-5
ISBN-10: 0-545-14233-4

Text copyright © 2009 by Marion Dane Bauer
Illustrations copyright © 2009 by Jamie Smith

12 11 10   14/0

Printed in the U.S.A.   40
First printing, December 2009

Book design by Jennifer Rinaldi Windau

Today people of all races celebrate
Martin Luther King, Jr. Day.

But when Dr. King was a boy, he couldn't even go to the same schools as white children.

He couldn't play in the same parks.

Or eat in the same restaurants.

He couldn't drink at the same water fountains
as white people.

But his mother always told him, "M. L., don't you ever forget that you are just as good as anybody."

Young Martin believed that.
He believed it so much that he grew up
to teach that message to the world.

Dr. King said, "You are just as good as anybody."
And many people believed him.

Black people sat quietly at lunch counters just to show they belonged there.

They refused to ride buses that made black people sit in the back.

They walked alone into schools to prove that black children
had a right to learn beside white children.

And because so many people believed Dr. King,
at last they changed this country's laws.

Children of all races now learn at the same schools.

They play in the same parks.

They sit wherever they like on buses.

They eat in the same restaurants.

They drink at the same water fountains.

Because of Martin Luther King, Jr., children of all races now walk together as sisters and brothers!